MAJOR LEAGUE
BASEBALL STADIUM
MEMORIES

BUCKET LIST JOURNAL

TO ALL 30 MLB STADIUMS

THIS JOURNAL BELONGS TO:

_____

Nothing says America like the smell of fresh cut grass, the crack of a wooden bat, and the sight of fireworks on a warm summer night—Baseball. Baseball is America's great pastime, and continues to be a deep-rooted part of our culture. Visiting each Major League ballpark will not only give you the opportunity to witness the worlds best athletes but also allow you to be immersed in the hearts of these great cities. Good luck on your trip across America!

BASEBALL STADIUMS

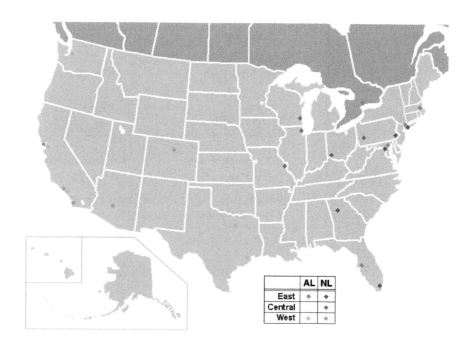

	AL	NL
East	◆	◆
Central		◆
West	◆	◆

ANGEL STADIUM
Anaheim, CA

Date Visited:

Weather

Temp:_____

Angels   Vs.   _____

Where I Sat

My Seat Number:

Stadium Description:

_____

_____

_____

What I Enjoyed Most At Angel Stadium:

_____

_____

_____

Best Part Of The Game:

_____

_____

Most Memorable Moment:

_____

_____

Favorite Player to Watch:

_____

Best Food:

_____

Other Things We Did In Anaheim:

_____

_____

Game Stats

	1	2	3	4	5	6	7	8	9			R	H	E
Visitor:														
Home: Angels														

Winning Pitcher: Losing Pitcher:

Tickets, Photos, And Autographs

BUSCH STADIUM
St. Louis, MO

Date Visited:

Weather

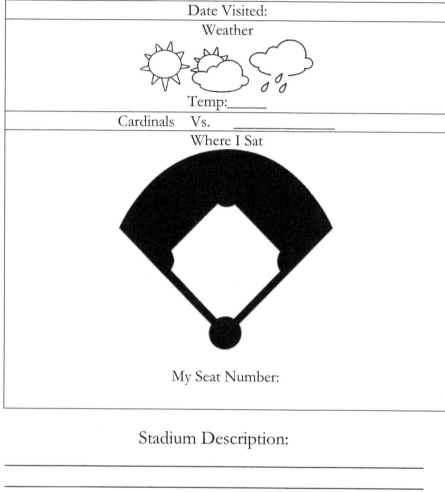

Temp:_____

Cardinals   Vs.   _____

Where I Sat

My Seat Number:

Stadium Description:

_____

_____

_____

What I Enjoyed Most At Busch Stadium:

_____

_____

_____

Best Part Of The Game:

_____

_____

Most Memorable Moment:

_____

_____

Favorite Player to Watch:

_____

Best Food:

_____

Other Things We Did In St. Louis:

_____

_____

Game Stats

	1	2	3	4	5	6	7	8	9			R	H	E
Visitor:														
Home: Cardinals														

Winning Pitcher: Losing Pitcher:

Tickets, Photos, and Autographs

CHASE FIELD
Phoenix, AZ

Date Visited:

Weather

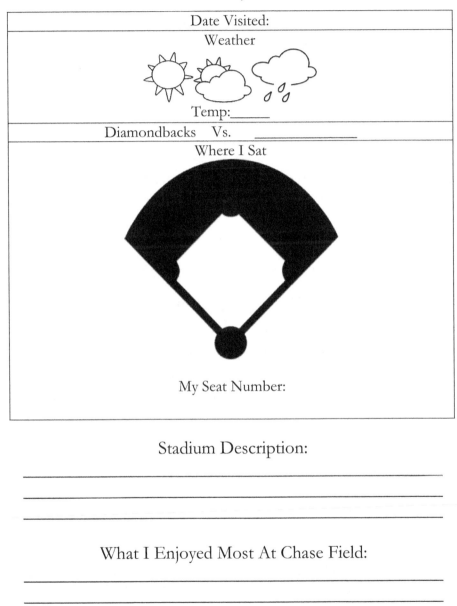

Temp:_____

Diamondbacks   Vs.   _____

Where I Sat

My Seat Number:

Stadium Description:

_____

_____

_____

What I Enjoyed Most At Chase Field:

_____

_____

_____

Best Part Of The Game:

_____

_____

Most Memorable Moment:

_____

_____

Favorite Player to Watch:

_____

Best Food:

_____

Other Things We Did In Phoenix:

_____

_____

Game Stats

	1	2	3	4	5	6	7	8	9		R	H	E
Visitor:													
Home: Diamondbacks													

Winning Pitcher:	Losing Pitcher:

Tickets, Photos, And Autographs

CITI FIELD
Queens, NY

Date Visited:

Weather

Temp:_____

Mets   Vs.   _____

Where I Sat

My Seat Number:

Stadium Description:

_____

_____

_____

What I Enjoyed Most At Citi Field:

_____

_____

_____

Best Part Of The Game:

_____

_____

Most Memorable Moment:

_____

_____

Favorite Player to Watch:

_____

Best Food:

_____

Other Things We Did In Queens:

_____

_____

Game Stats

	1	2	3	4	5	6	7	8	9			R	H	E
Visitor:														
Home: Mets														

Winning Pitcher: Losing Pitcher:

Tickets, Photos, And Autographs

CITIZENS BANK PARK
Philadelphia, PA

Date Visited:

Weather

Temp:_____

Phillies   Vs.   _____

Where I Sat

My Seat Number:

Stadium Description:

_____

_____

_____

What I Enjoyed Most At Citizens Bank Park:

_____

_____

_____

Best Part Of The Game:

_____

_____

Most Memorable Moment:

_____

_____

Favorite Player to Watch:

_____

Best Food:

_____

Other Things We Did In Philadelphia:

_____

_____

Game Stats

	1	2	3	4	5	6	7	8	9			R	H	E
Visitor:														
Home: Phillies														
	Winning Pitcher:						Losing Pitcher:							

Tickets, Photos, And Autographs

COMERICA PARK
Detroit, MI

Date Visited:
Weather
Temp:_____
Tigers   Vs.   _____
Where I Sat
My Seat Number:

Stadium Description:

_____

_____

_____

What I Enjoyed Most At Comerica Park:

_____

_____

_____

Best Part Of The Game:

_____

_____

Most Memorable Moment:

_____

_____

Favorite Player to Watch:

_____

Best Food:

_____

Other Things We Did In Detroit:

_____

_____

Game Stats

	1	2	3	4	5	6	7	8	9			R	H	E
Visitor:														
Home: Tigers														
Winning Pitcher:							Losing Pitcher:							

Tickets, Photos, And Autographs

COORS FIELD
Denver, CO

Date Visited:

Weather

Temp:_____

Rockies   Vs.   _____

Where I Sat

My Seat Number:

Stadium Description:

_____

_____

_____

What I Enjoyed Most At Coors Field:

_____

_____

_____

Best Part Of The Game:

_____

_____

Most Memorable Moment:

_____

_____

Favorite Player to Watch:

_____

Best Food:

_____

Other Things We Did In Denver:

_____

_____

Game Stats

	1	2	3	4	5	6	7	8	9			R	H	E
Visitor:														
Home: Rockies														
	Winning Pitcher:							Losing Pitcher:						

Tickets, Photos, And Autographs

DODGER STADIUM
Los Angeles, CA

Date Visited:
Weather
Temp:_____
Dodgers   Vs.   _____
Where I Sat
My Seat Number:

Stadium Description:

_____

_____

_____

What I Enjoyed Most At Dodger Stadium:

_____

_____

_____

Best Part Of The Game:

_____

_____

Most Memorable Moment:

_____

_____

Favorite Player to Watch:

_____

Best Food:

_____

Other Things We Did In Los Angeles:

_____

_____

Game Stats

	1	2	3	4	5	6	7	8	9			R	H	E
Visitor:														
Home: Dodgers														
	Winning Pitcher:							Losing Pitcher:						

Tickets, Photos, And Autographs

FENWAY PARK
Boston, MA

Date Visited:
Weather

Temp:_____

Red Sox   Vs.   _____

Where I Sat

My Seat Number:

Stadium Description:

_____

_____

_____

What I Enjoyed Most At Fenway Park:

_____

_____

Best Part Of The Game:

_____

_____

Most Memorable Moment:

_____

_____

Favorite Player to Watch:

_____

Best Food:

_____

Other Things We Did In Boston:

_____

_____

Game Stats

	1	2	3	4	5	6	7	8	9			R	H	E
Visitor:														
Home: Red Sox														
Winning Pitcher:						Losing Pitcher:								

Tickets, Photos, And Autographs

GLOBE LIFE PARK
Arlington, TX

Date Visited:
Weather
Temp:_____
Rangers   Vs.   _____
Where I Sat
My Seat Number:

Stadium Description:

_____

_____

_____

What I Enjoyed Most At Globe Life Park:

_____

_____

Best Part Of The Game:

_____

_____

Most Memorable Moment:

_____

_____

Favorite Player to Watch:

_____

Best Food:

_____

Other Things We Did In Arlington:

_____

_____

Game Stats

	1	2	3	4	5	6	7	8	9			R	H	E
Visitor:														
Home: Rangers														
	Winning Pitcher:							Losing Pitcher:						

Tickets, Photos, And Autographs

GREAT AMERICAN BALLPARK
Cincinnati, OH

Date Visited:
Weather

Temp:_____

Reds   Vs. _____

Where I Sat

My Seat Number:

Stadium Description:

_____

_____

_____

What I Enjoyed Most At Great American Ballpark:

_____

_____

_____

Best Part Of The Game:

_____

_____

Most Memorable Moment:

_____

_____

Favorite Player to Watch:

_____

Best Food:

_____

Other Things We Did In Cincinnati:

_____

_____

Game Stats

	1	2	3	4	5	6	7	8	9			R	H	E
Visitor:														
Home: Reds														
	Winning Pitcher:							Losing Pitcher:						

36

Tickets, Photos, And Autographs

GUARANTEED RATE FIELD
Chicago, IL

Date Visited:
Weather
Temp:_____
White Sox   Vs.   _____
Where I Sat
My Seat Number:

Stadium Description:

_____

_____

_____

What I Enjoyed Most At Guaranteed Rate Field:

_____

_____

_____

Best Part Of The Game:

_____

_____

Most Memorable Moment:

_____

_____

Favorite Player to Watch:

_____

Best Food:

_____

Other Things We Did In Chicago:

_____

_____

Game Stats

	1	2	3	4	5	6	7	8	9			R	H	E
Visitor:														
Home: White Sox														

Winning Pitcher: Losing Pitcher:

Tickets, Photos, And Autographs

KAUFFMAN STADIUM
Kansas City, MO

Date Visited:
Weather 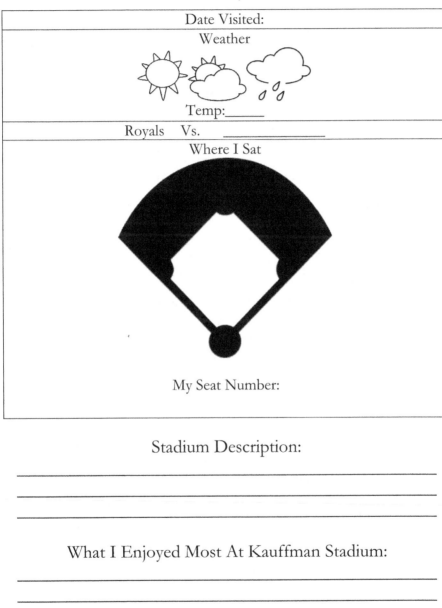 Temp:_____
Royals   Vs.   _____
Where I Sat
My Seat Number:

Stadium Description:

_____

_____

_____

What I Enjoyed Most At Kauffman Stadium:

_____

_____

_____

Best Part Of The Game:

_____

_____

Most Memorable Moment:

_____

_____

Favorite Player to Watch:

_____

Best Food:

_____

Other Things We Did In Kansas City:

_____

_____

Game Stats

	1	2	3	4	5	6	7	8	9			R	H	E
Visitor:														
Home: Royals														

Winning Pitcher:	Losing Pitcher:

Tickets, Photos, And Autographs

MARLINS PARK
Miami, FL

Date Visited:
Weather

Temp:_____

Marlins   Vs.   _____

Where I Sat

My Seat Number:

Stadium Description:

_____

_____

_____

What I Enjoyed Most At Marlins Park:

_____

_____

_____

Best Part Of The Game:

_____

_____

Most Memorable Moment:

_____

_____

Favorite Player to Watch:

_____

Best Food:

_____

Other Things We Did In Miami:

_____

_____

Game Stats

	1	2	3	4	5	6	7	8	9			R	H	E
Visitor:														
Home: Marlins														
	Winning Pitcher:						Losing Pitcher:							

Tickets, Photos, And Autographs

MILLER PARK
Milwaukee, WI

Date Visited:
Weather

Temp:_____

Brewers   Vs.   _____

Where I Sat

My Seat Number:

Stadium Description:

_____
_____
_____

What I Enjoyed Most At Miller Park:

_____
_____

Best Part Of The Game:

_____

_____

Most Memorable Moment:

_____

_____

Favorite Player to Watch:

_____

Best Food:

_____

Other Things We Did In Milwaukee:

_____

_____

Game Stats

	1	2	3	4	5	6	7	8	9			R	H	E
Visitor:														
Home: Brewers														

Winning Pitcher: Losing Pitcher:

Tickets, Photos, And Autographs

MINUTE MAID PARK
Houston, TX

Date Visited:
Weather

Temp:_____

Astros   Vs.   _____

Where I Sat

My Seat Number:

Stadium Description:

_____

_____

_____

What I Enjoyed Most At Minute Maid Park:

_____

_____

_____

Best Part Of The Game:

_____

_____

Most Memorable Moment:

_____

_____

Favorite Player to Watch:

_____

Best Food:

_____

Other Things We Did In Houston:

_____

_____

Game Stats

	1	2	3	4	5	6	7	8	9		R	H	E
Visitor:													
Home: Astros													
Winning Pitcher:					Losing Pitcher:								

Tickets, Photos, And Autographs

NATIONALS PARK
Washington, D.C.

Date Visited:

Weather

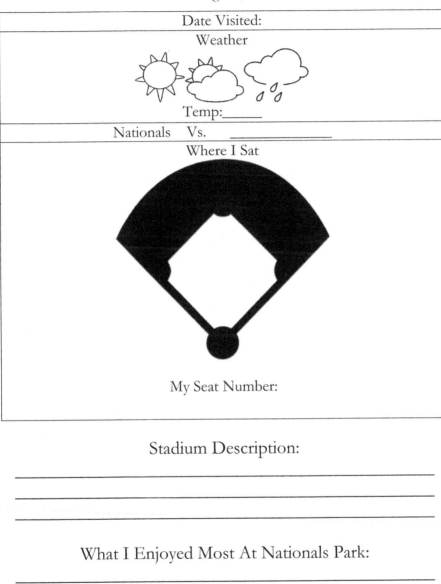

Temp:_____

Nationals   Vs.   _____

Where I Sat

My Seat Number:

Stadium Description:

_____

_____

_____

What I Enjoyed Most At Nationals Park:

_____

_____

_____

Best Part Of The Game:

_____

_____

Most Memorable Moment:

_____

_____

Favorite Player to Watch:

_____

Best Food:

_____

Other Things We Did In Washington D.C.:

_____

_____

Game Stats

	1	2	3	4	5	6	7	8	9			R	H	E
Visitor:														
Home: Nationals														
Winning Pitcher:						Losing Pitcher:								

Tickets, Photos, And Autographs

ALAMEDA COUNTY COLISEUM
Oakland, CA

Date Visited:
Weather
Temp:_____
Athletics   Vs.   _____
Where I Sat
My Seat Number:

Stadium Description:

_____

_____

_____

What I Enjoyed Most At Alameda County Coliseum:

_____

_____

_____

Best Part Of The Game:

_____

_____

Most Memorable Moment:

_____

_____

Favorite Player to Watch:

_____

Best Food:

_____

Other Things We Did In Oakland:

_____

_____

Game Stats

	1	2	3	4	5	6	7	8	9			R	H	E
Visitor:														
Home: Athletics														
	Winning Pitcher:							Losing Pitcher:						

Tickets, Photos, And Autographs

ORACLE PARK
San Francisco, CA

Date Visited:
Weather

Temp:_____

Giants   Vs.   _____

Where I Sat

My Seat Number:

Stadium Description:

_____

_____

_____

What I Enjoyed Most At Oracle Park:

_____

_____

_____

Best Part Of The Game:

_____

_____

Most Memorable Moment:

_____

_____

Favorite Player to Watch:

_____

Best Food:

_____

Other Things We Did In San Francisco:

_____

_____

Game Stats

	1	2	3	4	5	6	7	8	9			R	H	E
Visitor:														
Home: Giants														
	Winning Pitcher:						Losing Pitcher:							

Tickets, Photos, And Autographs

CAMDEN YARDS
Baltimore, MD

Date Visited:
Weather
Temp:_____
Orioles   Vs.   _____

Where I Sat

My Seat Number:

Stadium Description:

_____

_____

_____

What I Enjoyed Most At Camden Yards:

_____

_____

_____

Best Part Of The Game:

_____

_____

Most Memorable Moment:

_____

_____

Favorite Player to Watch:

_____

Best Food:

_____

Other Things We Did In Baltimore:

_____

_____

Game Stats

	1	2	3	4	5	6	7	8	9			R	H	E
Visitor:														
Home: Orioles														
	Winning Pitcher:						Losing Pitcher:							

Tickets, Photos, And Autographs

PETCO PARK
San Diego, CA

Date Visited:

Weather

Temp:_____

Padres   Vs.   _____

Where I Sat

My Seat Number:

Stadium Description:

_____

_____

_____

What I Enjoyed Most At Petco Park:

_____

_____

_____

Best Part Of The Game:

_____

_____

Most Memorable Moment:

_____

_____

Favorite Player to Watch:

_____

Best Food:

_____

Other Things We Did In San Diego:

_____

_____

Game Stats

	1	2	3	4	5	6	7	8	9			R	H	E
Visitor:														
Home: Padres														
	Winning Pitcher:					Losing Pitcher:								

Tickets, Photos, And Autographs

PNC PARK
Pittsburgh, PA

Date Visited:
Weather

Temp:_____

Pirates   Vs.   _____

Where I Sat

My Seat Number:

Stadium Description:

_____

_____

_____

What I Enjoyed Most At PNC Park:

_____

_____

Best Part Of The Game:

_____

_____

Most Memorable Moment:

_____

_____

Favorite Player to Watch:

_____

Best Food:

_____

Other Things We Did In Pittsburgh:

_____

_____

Game Stats

	1	2	3	4	5	6	7	8	9			R	H	E
Visitor:														
Home: Pirates														
	Winning Pitcher:						Losing Pitcher:							

Tickets, Photos, And Autographs

PROGRESSIVE FIELD
Cleveland, OH

Date Visited:

Weather

Temp:_____

Indians   Vs.   _____

Where I Sat

My Seat Number:

Stadium Description:

_____
_____
_____

What I Enjoyed Most At Progressive Field:

_____
_____
_____

Best Part Of The Game:

_____

_____

Most Memorable Moment:

_____

_____

Favorite Player to Watch:

_____

Best Food:

_____

Other Things We Did In Cleveland:

_____

_____

Game Stats

	1	2	3	4	5	6	7	8	9			R	H	E
Visitor:														
Home: Indians														
	Winning Pitcher:					Losing Pitcher:								

Tickets, Photos, And Autographs

ROGERS CENTRE
Toronto, Ontario

Date Visited:
Weather
Temp:_____
Blue Jays   Vs.   _____
Where I Sat
My Seat Number:

Stadium Description:

_____

_____

_____

What I Enjoyed Most At Rogers Centre:

_____

_____

Best Part Of The Game:

_____

_____

Most Memorable Moment:

_____

_____

Favorite Player to Watch:

_____

Best Food:

_____

Other Things We Did In Toronto:

_____

_____

Game Stats

	1	2	3	4	5	6	7	8	9			R	H	E
Visitor:														
Home: Blue Jays														
	Winning Pitcher:						Losing Pitcher:							

Tickets, Photos, And Autographs

SUNTRUST PARK
Cumberland, GA

Date Visited:

Weather

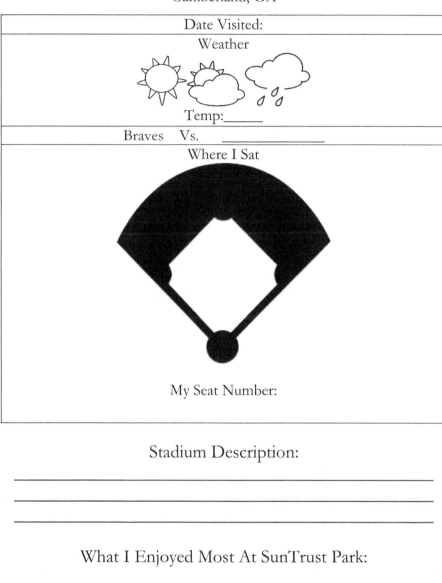

Temp:_____

Braves   Vs.   _____

Where I Sat

My Seat Number:

Stadium Description:

_____

_____

_____

What I Enjoyed Most At SunTrust Park:

_____

_____

_____

Best Part Of The Game:

_____

_____

Most Memorable Moment:

_____

_____

Favorite Player to Watch:

_____

Best Food:

_____

Other Things We Did In Atlanta:

_____

_____

Game Stats

	1	2	3	4	5	6	7	8	9			R	H	E
Visitor:														
Home: Braves														

Winning Pitcher: Losing Pitcher:

Tickets, Photos, And Autographs

T-MOBILE PARK
Seattle, WA

Date Visited:
Weather
Temp:_____
Mariners   Vs.   _____
Where I Sat
My Seat Number:

Stadium Description:

_____

_____

_____

What I Enjoyed Most At T-Mobile Park:

_____

_____

_____

Best Part Of The Game:

_____

_____

Most Memorable Moment:

_____

_____

Favorite Player to Watch:

_____

Best Food:

_____

Other Things We Did In Seattle:

_____

_____

Game Stats

	1	2	3	4	5	6	7	8	9			R	H	E
Visitor:														
Home: Mariners														
	Winning Pitcher:						Losing Pitcher:							

Tickets, Photos, And Autographs

TARGET FIELD
Minneapolis, MN

Date Visited:
Weather

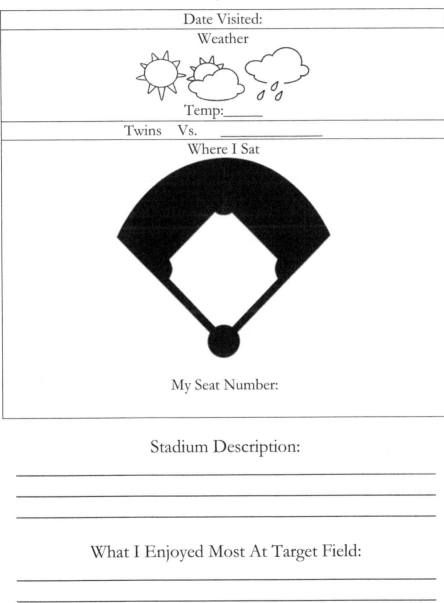

Temp:_____

Twins   Vs.   _____

Where I Sat

My Seat Number:

Stadium Description:

_____

_____

_____

What I Enjoyed Most At Target Field:

_____

_____

_____

Best Part Of The Game:

_____

_____

Most Memorable Moment:

_____

_____

Favorite Player to Watch:

_____

Best Food:

_____

Other Things We Did In Minneapolis:

_____

_____

Game Stats

	1	2	3	4	5	6	7	8	9		R	H	E
Visitor:													
Home: Twins													
Winning Pitcher:					Losing Pitcher:								

Tickets, Photos, And Autographs

TROPICANA FIELD
St. Petersburg, FL

Date Visited:
Weather
Temp:_____
Rays Vs. _____
Where I Sat
My Seat Number:

Stadium Description:

_____

_____

_____

What I Enjoyed Most At Tropicana Field:

_____

_____

_____

Best Part Of The Game:

_____

_____

Most Memorable Moment:

_____

_____

Favorite Player to Watch:

_____

Best Food:

_____

Other Things We Did In St. Petersburg:

_____

_____

Game Stats

	1	2	3	4	5	6	7	8	9			R	H	E
Visitor:														
Home: Rays														
	Winning Pitcher:							Losing Pitcher:						

Tickets, Photos, And Autographs

WRIGLEY FIELD
Chicago, IL

| Date Visited: |
| Weather |
| Temp:_____ |
| Cubs   Vs.   _____ |
| Where I Sat |

My Seat Number:

Stadium Description:

_____

_____

_____

What I Enjoyed Most At Wrigley Field:

_____

_____

_____

Best Part Of The Game:

_____

_____

Most Memorable Moment:

_____

_____

Favorite Player to Watch:

_____

Best Food:

_____

Other Things We Did In Chicago:

_____

_____

Game Stats

	1	2	3	4	5	6	7	8	9		R	H	E
Visitor:													
Home: Cubs													
	Winning Pitcher:						Losing Pitcher:						

Tickets, Photos, And Autographs

YANKEE STADIUM
Bronx, NY

Date Visited:
Weather
Temp:_____
Yankees   Vs.   _____
Where I Sat
My Seat Number:

Stadium Description:

_____

_____

_____

What I Enjoyed Most At Yankee Stadium:

_____

_____

_____

Best Part Of The Game:

_____

_____

Most Memorable Moment:

_____

_____

Favorite Player to Watch:

_____

Best Food:

_____

Other Things We Did In the Bronx:

_____

_____

Game Stats

	1	2	3	4	5	6	7	8	9			R	H	E
Visitor:														
Home: Yankees														
	Winning Pitcher:					Losing Pitcher:								

Tickets, Photos, And Autographs

Made in United States
North Haven, CT
13 March 2023